Japan

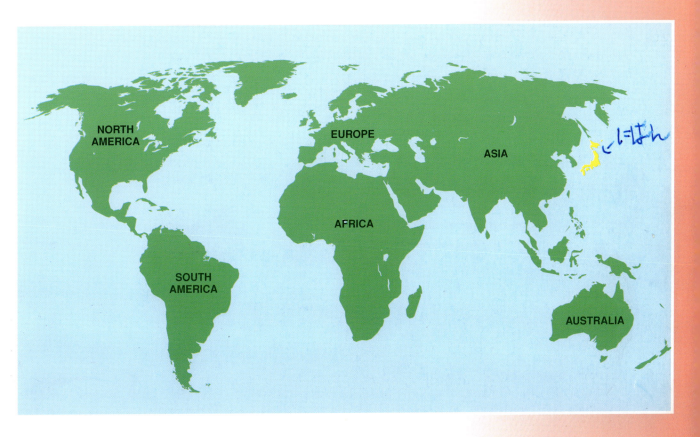

にほん

Clare Boast

First published in Great Britain by Heinemann Library
Halley Court, Jordan Hill, Oxford OX2 8EJ
a division of Reed Educational and Professional Publishing Ltd

OXFORD FLORENCE PRAGUE MADRID ATHENS
MELBOURNE AUCKLAND KUALA LUMPUR SINGAPORE TOKYO
IBADAN NAIROBI KAMPALA JOHANNESBURG GABORONE
PORTSMOUTH NH CHICAGO MEXICO CITY SAO PAULO

Designed by AMR
Illustrations by Art Construction
Printed and bound in Italy by L.E.G.O

01 00 99 98 97
10 9 8 7 6 5 4 3 2 1

ISBN 0 431 04548 8

British Library Cataloguing in Publication Data

Boast, Clare
Step into Japan
1. Japan – Geography – Juvenile literature
I. Title II. Japan
915.2

Acknowledgements
The Publishers would like to thank the following for permission to reproduce photographs:
J Allan Cash Ltd, pp.10, 19, 24; Colorific! H. Aga p.25, B. Martin p.8, H. Sautter p.23; Robert Harding Picture Library Ltd p.29; Trip: Trip pp.12, 13, 14, 16, 17, 21, Art Directors p.26, J. Dakers p.6, J. Holmes p.15, T. Morse pp.27-8, P. Rauter pp.18, 22, C. Rennie pp.4, 5, 9, 11, A. Tovy pp.6, 22.

Cover photograph reproduced with permission of:
    child: Image Bank, Stephen Marks
    background: Tony Stone Images, Yann Layma.

Our thanks to Betty Root for her comments in the preparation of this book.

Every effort has been made to contact copyright holders of any material reproduced in this book. Any omissions will be rectified in subsequent printings if notice is given to the Publisher.

CONTENTS

INTRODUCTION

WHERE IS JAPAN?

Japan is made up of over 4000 **islands**. These islands stretch out in a line in the Pacific Ocean. Most of the 125 million people live on the four biggest islands: Hokkaido, Honshu, Shikoku and Kyushu.

Hiroshima was bombed in 1945. This building was left unrepaired as a reminder of the people who died.

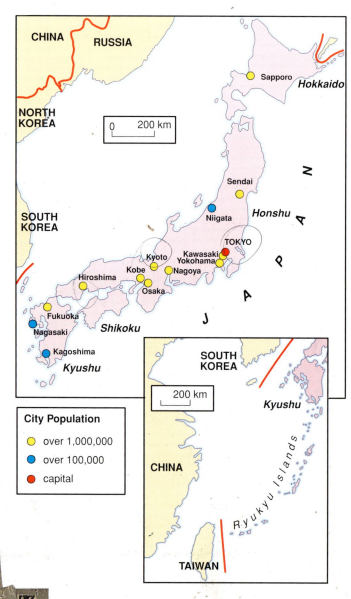

CHINA
RUSSIA
NORTH KOREA
SOUTH KOREA
Sapporo *Hokkaido*
0   200 km
Sendai
Niigata   *Honshu*
Kyoto   Kawasaki   TOKYO
Kobe   Yokohama
Hiroshima   Nagoya
Osaka
Fukuoka
Nagasaki   *Shikoku*
Kagoshima
Kyushu

City Population
- 🟡 over 1,000,000
- 🔵 over 100,000
- 🔴 capital

SOUTH KOREA
200 km
Kyushu
CHINA
Ryukyu Islands
TAIWAN

JAPAN'S HISTORY

Japan was ruled at first by warriors, then **emperors**. These rulers did not want to have anything to do with other countries. But by 100 years ago, Japan was trading with other countries. It then fought in the Second World War, which ended in 1945 when the first **atomic bomb** was dropped on Hiroshima.

Today, Japan is a peaceful country. It is also very rich. Japan makes a lot of **goods**, especially electrical goods, to sell all over the world.

The Japanese call their country 'Nippon' which means 'land of the rising sun'.

The Golden Pavilion in Kyoto (on Honshu) was built in 1397. It is a temple for one of the religions in Japan, Buddhism.

THE LAND

Japan has a lot of earthquakes. These homes in Kobe were hit by an earthquake in 1995.

MOUNTAINS AND VALLEYS

Most of Japan is covered with steep mountains. Streams and rivers that run down from these mountains to the sea have made deep valleys. The rivers often flood in the rainy season, or when the snow melts on the mountains in summer.

This mountain is called Mount Fuji. It is a volcano, but it has not erupted for many years.

PLAINS

Some of the land is flat. These flat plains are at the bottom of the valleys and along the **coast**.

VOLCANOES

Many of Japan's mountains are **volcanoes**. They can erupt, throwing out ash and rocks which rain down on places nearby. Volcanoes also pour out **lava** which flows down the mountain, burning everything in its way.

EARTHQUAKES

Japan also has earthquakes, which make the ground shake. Earthquakes can be small, but big earthquakes can destroy buildings and roads and kill a lot of people.

Japan can have up to three small earthquakes each day. Buildings are made to move with these small earthquakes.

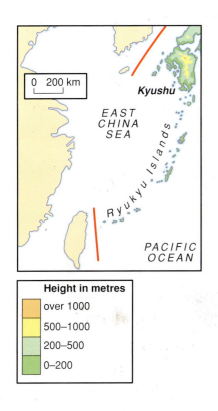

WEATHER, PLANTS AND ANIMALS

THE WEATHER

The north and south of Japan are far apart, so the weather is very different.

The north is colder than the south and has lots of snow. In the south it is warm all year round.

Most of Japan has a 'rainy season' between June and September. It rains hard almost every day. In September there are often strong winds called **typhoons**.

Hardly anyone goes outside in the rainy season in Japan without an umbrella!

Tourists are taken up Mount Fuji by cable car. Trees cover the parts of the mountains that are too steep to farm.

PLANTS AND ANIMALS

The plants in Japan change from north to the south. They change as you go higher up, too. In the south there are plants and trees that like hot, wet weather. They could not grow in the north. There are fir trees in the mountains, but oak and maple trees grow lower down. The flat land has been cleared for farming and industry.

There are lots of wild animals in Japan. You can find monkeys, bears, foxes and poisonous snakes.

In Japan, there is a sort of lizard (called a salamander) that grows up to 1.5 m long.

9

TOWNS AND CITIES

A busy street in Tokyo. The bridge is for trains, which run over the roads to use less space.

TOKYO

Tokyo is the **capital city** of Japan. About 12 million people live there. It is a modern city with universities, theatres, museums, libraries, offices and shops.

Much of old Tokyo was destroyed by an earthquake in 1923. It was rebuilt, but was destroyed by bombing during the Second World War. After this, Tokyo's buildings were rebuilt to move with earthquakes, so they would not fall down.

OTHER TOWNS AND CITIES

All of Japan's cities and towns are very crowded. Many of them are built on the narrow, flat plains between the high mountains and the sea. There is not much space for cities and towns to grow, and lots of people want to live there. Homes are usually small.

MAKING MORE SPACE

Some cities are so short of space that they have filled the sea with rocks and built on this land. Osaka's airport is built out into the sea.

People built tall buildings to save space. Some cities make builders pay a 'sunshine tax' if new buildings block out the sun from old ones.

Nagasaki squeezes in between the mountains and the sea. About 450,000 people live there.

LIVING IN TOKYO

THE SHISHIDO FAMILY

Hajime and Junko Shishido live in Tokyo. They have one girl, Emi (who is 13) and one boy, Yuta (who is 10). The children's grandparents, Tadao and Fumi, live there too. In Japan, most grandparents live with the family.

The family live in a house on the edge of Tokyo. It has five rooms but there is no space for a garden.

THE FAMILY'S DAY

Hajime and Junko work all week. Junko stops work at 2 pm, but Hajime often works in his office until 9 pm. The children go to school, while their grandparents stay at home and help with the housework.

The family can eat their evening meal together at weekends.

Yuta goes to school at 7 am. He comes back at 3 pm.

MEAL TIMES

Junko does most of her food shopping in the supermarket on her way home from work. The family eat a lot of noodles, rice, meat, fish and vegetables. They also like steak and sushi (raw fish served with rice and vegetables).

Junko buys most of her food at the supermarket.

After the evening meal, Emi goes out to another school. She is working for exams. She gets home at 10 pm.

The underground train is the quickest way for Hajime to get to work.

13

FARMING IN JAPAN

There are not many farms in Japan. The weather is good for growing crops. But the land is either too steep to farm, or has cities and factories built on it.

CROPS

Japan's main crop is rice. Rice is grown in paddy fields. For some of its growing time, rice has to be kept underwater. Farmers also grow vegetables like onions, potatoes and cabbages. They grow oranges, too.

The banks around these rice fields hold in the water when it is needed.

Although there is not much farm land, Japan grows about 60% of all the food it needs by careful farming.

Fish is an important food in Japan, and there are about 27,000 fishing boats in the country.

FAMILY FARMS

Most farms are small and owned by one family. Everyone in the family works on the farm, even the children. They have to make the best use of every bit of land. They use lots of **fertilizers** and spend a lot of time weeding the crops. They use special small tractors and other farm machines.

Some farmers run fish farms, where they breed fish for food.

LIVING IN THE COUNTRY

The Yonezumi family outside their farmhouse. Seiji has already gone to work.

THE YONEZUMI FAMILY

Seiji and Mariko Yonezumi work on a small farm. They have three boys, Tomoaki (who is 12) Matsataka (who is nine) and Naochika (who is six). The children's grandparents, Kiyo and Toshikazu, live there too.

WORK ON THE FARM

The grandparents do most of the work on the farm. The farm does not make enough for the family to live on, so Seiji and Mariko both go out to work.

The family eat their meal off a low table. They sit on the floor.

Kiyo working in the fields. She is wearing typical work clothes, which allow her to move easily and the hat protects her from the sun.

THE CHILDREN'S DAY

Tomoaki and Matsataka have to walk more than 2 km to get to school. Tomoaki has to leave for school at 7.30 am. On Fridays he goes from one school to another school, to have extra lessons. Naochika goes to a nursery school.

The children like to watch TV and play games on their computer. They also like playing football with the other children in the village.

A football makes the walk to school more fun for Tomoaki.

JAPANESE SHOPS

DAILY SHOPPING

Japan has small shops and local markets where people can buy food each day. Farmers bring fruit and vegetables to market and people sell live fish, swimming in water tanks, so people know they are fresh.

More and more Japanese people buy food from supermarkets. More women work full-time, and have to shop on their way home. Supermarkets are quick and easy.

Market stalls are a good place to buy fresh local food, like these vegetables.

Japan is famous for its electrical goods. Most Japanese homes have computers, washing machines, TVs and cookers.

CITY SHOPPING

Japanese cities have lots of shops selling electrical **goods** and other expensive things, like clothes. People buy smart things to wear for work. Young people like to wear jeans. Japanese people only wear traditional Japanese clothes on special occasions.

Kimonos are traditional Japanese dresses. They cost a lot because they are made by hand. They take about 20 minutes to put on!

JAPANESE FOOD

RICE AND VEGETABLES

Japanese people eat rice and vegetables with most of their meals. Vegetables are often cooked by chopping them up and frying them quickly. This way of cooking is called stir-frying.

People use lots of soya bean paste and soya sauce in cooking.

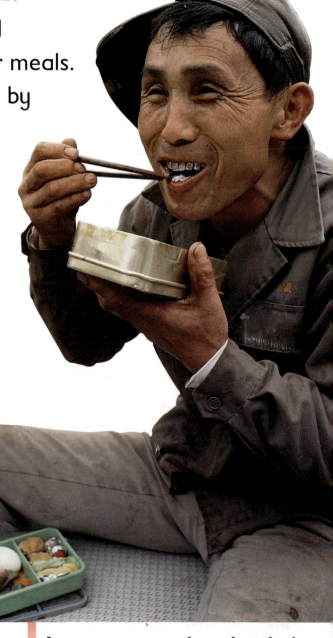

Japanese people take their lunch to work, packed in a special box, called a bento. They usually eat with chopsticks.

These men in a Tokyo fish market are cutting up tuna.

FISH AND MEAT

There are lots of different sorts of fish and seafood in the Pacific Ocean. So fish is an important part of Japanese cooking. Fish can be eaten raw with sauces or rice – this is called sushi. But fish is also fried, grilled and baked.

People eat much less meat than fish. Most meat is cut into thin strips and cooked with vegetables and **noodles**.

Blowfish tastes good, but has a poisonous part that has to be carefully cut out. If any is left in, it can kill you!

MADE IN JAPAN

Japan sells all sorts of **goods** to other countries, especially electrical goods. Goods that are sold to other countries are called exports.

FACTORIES

Japanese factories make cars and motor bikes. They make electrical goods like computers, TVs, videos, CD players, cameras, watches and calculators.

Factories make a lot of smoke, which causes air **pollution** in nearby cities.

WORKERS

Japanese companies expect workers to work hard. Many workers stay with the same company for all their working lives. It is like a family. The company helps them to buy a home, makes sure they are looked after if they are sick and even helps with the children's education. It encourages everyone to work together as part of the company team.

Now this is changing. Many younger workers move about much more, looking for better jobs and pay.

More cars are made in Japan than in any other country in the world.

Many Japanese car factories use robots to put the cars together. People check the work at the end.

GETTING AROUND

Japanese cities have lots of traffic. Tokyo has traffic jams every day.

Travel is difficult in Japan because of the high mountains and many islands. But the main islands are now linked by road or rail bridges and tunnels.

ROADS

Japan has a motorway system which links all the main cities. There are long tunnels under the mountains. In the city, roads are very busy and traffic **pollution** makes the air bad to breathe. Some people wear face masks when walking or cycling.

RAILWAYS

The fastest way to travel on land in Japan is by the 'bullet train'. It links Tokyo and Osaka and travels at 270 kilometres per hour. Other cities are also linked by fast trains. The quick way to travel in cities is by underground railway.

Over 2.5 million people use just one of Tokyo's railway stations each day.

Station workers push people into Tokyo underground trains at busy times!

SPORTS AND HOLIDAYS

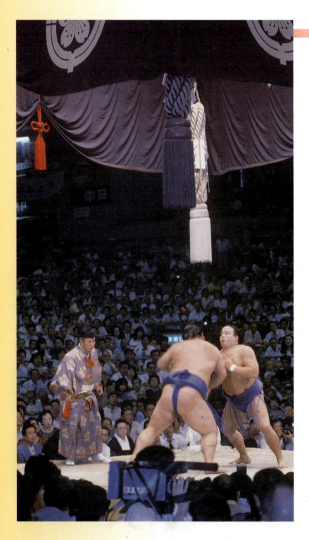

A sumo wrestling match. The best wrestlers are treated like film stars in Japan.

SPORTS

One of the most famous Japanese sports is sumo wrestling. Sumo wrestlers try to throw each other out of a ring.

Other popular sports are **martial arts** like judo and kendo. Baseball, football, swimming and basketball are popular. So is golf, but there are not many golf courses, because there is not enough flat land to build them on.

People like to visit local parks. They are full of cherry blossom in the spring.

TIME OFF

Traditional Japanese hobbies include origami (making folded paper shapes) and flower arranging. Young people prefer karaoke (singing to a music tape) and playing computer games. People also visit religious shrines and enjoy walking in parks and gardens.

HOLIDAYS

Many people come from all over the world to visit Japan. They visit the busy cities, the religious shrines and Mount Fuji. Many Japanese people go to other countries for their holidays.

The 1998 Winter Olympics will be held in Japan. There is lots of winter snow in the mountains.

FESTIVALS AND CUSTOMS

SPECIAL DAYS

There are lots of days off for special occasions in Japan. These include days when children or old people are given special treats, and the **emperor's** birthday. There are also New Year celebrations which go on for three days.

RELIGIOUS FESTIVALS

Japan has two main religions, Shintoism (where nature and ancestors are important) and Buddhism (where people follow the teachings of Buddha). Both religions have lots of festivals.

At this winter festival in Osaka men show how brave they are by not wearing clothes!

These women are making tea in a special **ceremony**. It can take four hours to make!

CUSTOMS

Many Japanese traditions are still important today. People like to watch Noh plays, about old battles and heroes. The Noh actors wear costumes and masks that have looked the same for hundreds of years. There is an old way of writing poetry (called haiku). The poems have only three lines. Japanese people also enjoy new things, like computer games or pop music.

JAPAN FACTFILE

People

People from Japan are called Japanese.

Population

There are 125 million people living in Japan.

Capital city

The capital city of Japan is Tokyo.

Money

Money in Japan is called the yen.

Largest cities

Tokyo is the largest city with nearly 12 million people. The second largest city is Yokohama. Osaka is the third largest city.

Language

People speak Japanese. The language is written from top to bottom and left to right.

Head of country

Japan has an **emperor** but it is ruled by a **government**.

Religion

Nearly all Japanese people belong to the Shinto and the Buddhist religions.

GLOSSARY

atomic bomb a very powerful bomb that destroys a lot of buildings and also affects the air, making people sick long after it has exploded

capital city where the government is based

ceremony an organized and formal way of doing things, often for religions or public occasions

coast where the land meets the sea

emperor the ruler of a country. The emperor of Japan used to make all the decisions. Now there is a government chosen by the Japanese people. The emperor is still head of the country, but does not have any real power.

fertilizer plant food

government people who run the country

goods things people make

island land with water all around it

lava melted rock from under the Earth's surface

martial art a type of fighting

noodles noodles are made from flour and water. They are shaped into long strands or ribbon's, then cooked.

pollution dirt in the air, water or on land

typhoons violent storms with strong winds and rain

volcano a mountain that sometimes throws out ash or melted rock

INDEX